T0197172

GOT QUESTIONS? BIBLE ANSWERS

REV. DR. HAIG KINOSIAN JR. D. D.

WESTBOW
P R E S S®
A DIVISION OF THOMAS NELSON
& ZONDERVAN

WestBow Press books may be ordered through booksellers or by contacting:

WestBow Press
A Division of Thomas Nelson & Zondervan
1663 Liberty Drive
Bloomington, IN 47403
www.westbowpress.com
1 (866) 928-1240

ISBN: 978-1-9736-6517-5 (sc)
ISBN: 978-1-9736-6516-8 (e)

Print information available on the last page.

WestBow Press rev. date: 06/11/2019

FOREWORD

These are Question by Christians, that are asked many times but never answered. I have decided to answer many of these question, that would help us as Christians, to have the full Armour of God on us in these days of warfare. The two Bibles I used: KJV, TLB. May the Lord, teach you and bless you.

11Timothy 2:15, 2Timothy 3:16

Trust Christ for Everything: Col. 2:-10

I am the Lord, there is None other. Isaiah45:5-8

We walk by Faith not by Sight. 2Cor. 5:7

Giving the Light of God to the World. 2Cor. 4:4-6

Your Speech with always Season. Col.4:6

You cannot over rule what God, Gives. Acts5:38-39

Obey God, not MAN. Acts 5:29-33

Natural Man does not understand the things of God, We as Christians do. 1Cor.2:10-16

God, overrides Satin, Satin, respects God. Job 1:6-12

Study the Word of God. 2Timothy 3:16

Our Substance is the Word of God, not bread. Math. 4:4

Cannot serve two Masters. Math. 6:24

Our Desire is to know Him, our Nutrition. Psalms. 63: 1-11

Ask, Seek, Knock, for the Answer. Math. 7:7

Watch who you give the Word of God, to. Math. 7:6

Judge not, that Ye be not Judge. Math. 1:5

God, will provide, Do not Worry. Math. 6:31-34

Demons, recognized Christ, Son of God. Luke 8:28

Sowing your Seed, in the wright place. Luke 8:5-8,12-15.

Nothing Covered, but All is revealed. Luke 12:2

Nothing is Hidden from God. Luke 8:17

God, gives us Wisdom and Understanding. Ephesian, 1:3,6,17-19,22,23.

Fellowship, and Treasures in Heaven. Ephesians 2:4-7

Christ. Returns for Us. Acts 1:9-12

Definition of the Word of God, and uses. Hebrews 4:12

Nothing Hidden from God. Hebrews 4:13

Conducts of Christians, in the Body of Christ. Col. 3:8-17.

Christ, is God, who Returns. Col. 3:4

Christ, the Fullness of God. Col.2:9-10

Jesus, is God. Rev. 1:7,8.

Which Gate Will you Enter? Math. 7:13-15.

Disobedience, Verses: Obedience. Romans 5:19

The Love of Money, Root of all Evil. 1Tim.1:10

You can not out give God. Luke 6:38

God, Owns All. Psalms 24:1

Wisdom of Man, Foolishness unto God.

1 Corinth.3:18-21

We are the Temple of God. 1 Corinth.3:16-17.

MAN, cannot heal, God, can without Hesitation. Acts 3:6-9.

The Holy Spirit, Poured out on Us. Acts 2:17

The purpose for the Body of Christ. Acts 2:42-47

God, is revealed to Mankind, No Excuse. Romans 1:18-25.

Man, has no excuse,they know that God, exist. Eccl. 3:11.14

Trust and Obey, Blessings and Rewards. Genesis 22:6-13

Be ye doer of the Word, not Hearers. James 1:22-25

Behold I stand at the Door, and Knock. Rev.3:20

Be still and listen to God. Psalm 46:10

The Purpose of the Church Body. Acts1:14

God Pours out His Spirit in the Last Days. Acts 2:16-20

The Holy Spirit, is God. Acts 5:3-4

Events of the End Times. 2Thess.2:2-15

Fathers teach your Kid, Love of Christ. Ephesians 6:4

God, is greater in us then the Adversary. 1John 4:4

The Fullness of God. Ephesians 3:16-19

Gentiles, are fellow heirs in the Body of Christ. Ephesians 3:6

God, does not Change. Malachi 3:6

Your Sins, separates us from the Love of God. Isaiah 59:2

Seared Conscience 1Timothy 4:2

Wisdom and Understanding. Ephesians 1:17-19,22,23

He has chosen us. Ephesians 1:4-6

Seek the Lord, while He may be Found. Isaiah 55:6-12

Set your affection on things Above. Col. 3:2

Fear the Lord, is the Beginning of Wisdom of God. Proverbs 9:10

The Comforter, is the H.S. For our benefit. John 14:26

The Father and Christ Are One. John 14:11

Nothing can Separate, From the Love of God. Roman 8:35-39

Christ, Predesignate us to be Sons of God.

Romans 8:29-32

The Holy Spirit, intercedes for us.

Romans 8:26,27

Christ, keeps His own Sheep. John 10:26-29

Right or Wrong Door, He knows our Voice.

John 10:1-5

Christ, prepares Mansions, for Us. John 14:1-4

A righteous man Availed Much. James 5:6

The Righteous, shall Flourish. Psalm 92.12

God, has not given us the Spirit of Fear. 2Timothy 1:7

When our Faith gives into Fear./Abraham. Gen.12:1-20

The Comforters, Purpose for us.

John 16:7,8,13,14

Christ, Prunes our Vines. John 15:1-7

Beware of false prophets 2 Peter 2:1-3

Satins, Punishment for Eternity. Rev. 20:10

False prophet Definition: Living Bible: 2Peter2:11

Behold, Christ Returns Quickly. Rev. 22:12-14

Not Works of Us, His Righteousness saved us. Titus. 3:5-7

We have many Members in Christ. Rom.12:1-2

Present your body a living Sacrifice. Rom.12:1-2

In the Beginning was the Word. John 1:1-5

For God, so Loved the World. John. 3:16-21

Confess with our Mouth,Believe. Rom.10:9-13

The Arm of God, over us. Isaiah 53:1-9

For unto us a Child is Born, A Son, Given.

Isaiah 9:6

Will a man Rob God? Malachi 3:8-10

Behold, we shall be like Him. 1. John 3:1-2

Who is Like the Lord. Exodus 15:11

Let the Peace of God, rule our lives. Col.3:15-17

Abraham, walked by Faith. Genesis 12:1-4

All things work for good for those in Christ. Roman 8:28

Gods, Perfection. Psalm 18:30

We Run, the Race to receive the Prize. 1 Corinthians. 9:24

Great is the Lord, To be Praised. Psalms 145:3,9

God, Knows, are Downs and Ups. Psalms 139:1-24

Walk in the middle of trouble, He will be Their. Psalms 139:7

Always Praise the Lord. Psalms 135:1-3

They that trust The Lord, Shall not be moved. Psalms 125:1

Your Help comes from the Lord. Psalms 121:1-8

Praise the Lord, all Nations. Psalms117:1,2

Fear of the Lord, is the Beginning of Wisdom. Psalms 111:10

Give Thanks to the Lord. Psalms 106:1

Make a joyful noise unto the Lord. Psalms 100:1-5

Come and Sing to the Lord. Psalms 95: 1-7

We should Hide in His, Refuge. Psalms 91:1-16

Call upon the Lord. Psalms 118:5,6,24,29

Keep His Commandments. Proverbs 3:1-6

Put on the Armor of God. Ephesians 6:11-19

Gods, purpose for Man. Ecclesiastes 12:13

Description, when You get Old. Ecclesiastes 12:1-7

The Builder of your Foundation. 1Corinth.3:10-16

Paul's, Persecution. 2 Corinthians 11:21-30

Define, False Prophet, NKJV: Jeremiah, 23:25-40

Define: False Prophecy. NKJV Deut: 13:1-5

Living Bible: Deut. 13:1-5

God, is Greater in You, Then the Adversary.

1 John.4:4

Jesus, and author, Finisher, of our Faith. Heb.12:2

All that Labor come to Him. Math.11:28

Responsibility, with Wealth. Ecclesiastes 5:18

Wisdom, Knowledge, and Riches. b2 Chronicles.1:11

Abuse what God, gives to Man. Ecclesiastes 6:1

Definition of a Bishop, or Pastor. Titus 1:7

Mockers, separate from God. Jude 1:17

Angels cast out because their Desire. Jude 1:6

Take the Right pathway or pay. 3 John 1:11

Stay on Solid Ground/don't change. 2Peter 3:17

God's time not ours. 2 Peter 3:8

The Lord knows how to deliver us. 2Peter2:9

True Prophecy, only comes from God.2Peter1:20

Humble yourself before God. 1Peter 5:6

If any man speaks, Speak the Oracles of God. 1 Peter 4:11

Finally, be of all One Mine. 1 Peter 3:8

Honor all men, Fear God. 1 Peter 2:17

The Word of the Lord, Endurance. 1 Peter 1:25

Be Ye Holy, for I Am Holy. 1 Peter 1:16

The Trials of your Faith, Are Precious.1Peter1:7

The Lord, is my Rock and my Fortress. Psalms 18:2

The Words of My Mouth be acceptable. Psalms 19:14

Fear Not, the Lord, is with You. Isaiah 41:10

Be Swift to Hear, Slow to Speak. James 1:19

Leave Parents, Cleave to Wife. Ephesians 5:31

Study the Word of God, Be prepared. 2 Tim.2:15

God's Faithfulness to Us. Joshua 1:5

The Prodigal Son. Luke 15:11

Marriage relationships and Commitment. Ephesian 5:22

Let no Man, deceive you with Vain Words. Ephesians 5:6

Be kind to One and another. Ephesians 4:32

Take off Old Nature, Put on the New nature. Ephesians 4:22

God's, gives us Gifts. Ephesians 4:11

Ask, Pray, Believe. Mark 11:24

No temptation, Taken you, its Common. 1 Corinthians 10:13

The Lord, is Faithful, and True. Deut. 7:9

God, will never Leave us, Forsake us. Heb.13:5

Man's Wisdom, Foolishness to God. 1Cor. 1:19

God, Seals us. 2 Cor. 1:21

We are made in His Image. Genesis 1:26

The Heaven Declare the Glory of God. Psalms 19:1

Let your Light shine before Men. Math.5:16

Draw Close to God. 4:7-8

Let Your Good Deeds be Seen. James 3:13-18

Don't Judge others. L.B. James 3:1-6

Faith without works is Dead. L.B. 2:17

What we say reveals who we are. L.B. 1:26-27

Your Identification, with the Lord, not World. L.B. James 1:9-11

Christ, Rules over the Adversary. Math.8:28

Speaking Lies in Hypocrisy. 1 Timothy 4:2

Lacking Wisdom of God, Ask. James 1:5

Obedience, to God's Word. Proverbs 4:1

Putting the Attributes, Word, Wisdom Etc. Proverbs 2:1

Those who are heavy Burden, go to God. Mathew 11:28

He makes the Barron Woman, be Joyful. Psalms 113:9

The Purpose and Function, body of Christ. Ephesians 4:1

Be Kind to one another. Ephesian 4:32

Put off the Old Nature. Ephesians 4:22

The Holy Spirit, be strong in the inner Man. Ephesians 3:6

Our Foundation, built on Christ. Ephesian 2:18

Saved through Grace by Faith. Ephesians 2:8

The Danger of the Human Tongue. James 3:5

Let God's Attributes, be shown through You. James 3:13

God, is not Mocked. Galatians 6:7

Behold I stand at the Door. Revelations 3:20

Same Mine, One to another. Romans 12:16

Nothing can Separate us from the love of God. Romans 8:38

Marriage. Mathew 19:5

Beginning of Wisdom, is the fear of the Lord. Psalms 111:10

Vengeance is the Lords. Romans 12:19

We all turn to Dust. Ecclesiastes. 3:20

Definition of a Prophet. Deuteronomy 13:1

Fear of the Lord. Proverbs 14:27

Mans, Ways to destruction. Proverbs 14:12

Seek toe Lord, while He may be found. Isaiah 55:6

Set your affection on things above. Col. 3:2

The fear of the Lord, beginning of Wisdom

Proverbs 9:10

The Comforter, H.S. Purpose for us. John 14:26

The Father and Christ, are One. John 14:11

Nothing can separate us from the Love of God Romans 8:35-39

Christ, Predesignate us to be Son's, of God.

Romans 8:29-32

The Holy Spirit, intercedes for us. Rom. 8:26-27

Christ, keeps His own Sheep. John 10:26-29

Right or Wrong Door, Christ, Knows are Voice. John 10:1-5

Christ, Prepares Mansions for Us. John 14:1-4

A righteous man Avail much. James 5:16

The Righteous Man, shall Flourish. Psalms92:12

God, has not given us the Spirit of Fear. 2Timothty 1:7

Abraham, testing of Faith. Genesis 12:1-20

The Comforter, purpose for Us. John 16:7,8,13,14

We are the Vine, Christ, prunes us. John 15:1-7

Behold, He Comes Quickly. Rev. 22:12-14

Not by Works of Righteousness, we have done. Titus 3:5,6.

Christians, Many members in One Body. Romans 12:4-8

Present Your Body a Living Sacrifice. Rom.12:1,2.

In the beginning, The Word, Existed.John 1:1-5

God, so Loved the World. John 3:16-21

Confession, Made with the Mouth. Rom. 10:9-13

The Arm of the Lord, revealed to us. Isaiah 53:1-9

Names of Christ. Isaiah 9:6

Will a man Rob God. Malachi 3:8-10

We shall be Like Him. 1John 3:1-2

Who is Like the Lord. Exodus 15:11

Peace of God, rule in your Heart. Col.3:15-17

Abraham, Walked by Faith. Genesis 12:1-4

Christians, All things worked together. Rom.8:28

God's Perfection. Psalms 18:30

Run the Race, Great Rewards.

1 Corinthians 9:24

Great is the Lord, Greatly to be Praise.

Psalms145:3,9

The Lord, understands are Ups, and Down. Psalms 139:1-24

Christ, is their, through are Walk. Psalms 138:7

Praise the Lord, always. Psalms 135:1-3

Trust, the Lord, always. Psalms 125:1

I will lift my eyes unto the Lord. Psalms. 121:1-8

O praise ye the Lord, all nations. Psalms117:1,2

Fear the Lord, beginning of Wisdom.

Psalms111:10

Praise the Lord, give Thanks. Psalms106:1

Make a Joyful Noise Unto the Lord.

Psalms 100:1-5

Oh Come and let us Sing unto the Lord.

Psalms 95:1-7

He that dwelleth in the Secret place of the Most Hi. Psalms 91:1-16

Call upon the Lord. Psalms 118:5,6,24,29

Forget not Gods Law. Proverbs 3:1-6

Put on the Whole Armor of God. Eph.6:11-19

Gods, purpose for man. Ecclesiastes 12:13

Description when you get Old.

Ecclesiastes 12:1-7

Your Foundation is Proven and Firm.

1 Corinthians 3L10-16

Paul's, Persecution. 2 Corinthians11:21-30

Definition of Prophesy

N.K.J.V. Jeremiah 23:25:40

False Prophesy. N.K.J.V. Deuteronomy13:1-5

False Prophesy, Define: T.L.B. 13:1

God's, is greater in You. 1 John4:4

Jesus, the Author, and Finisher of your Faith. Hebrews 12:2

Come unto me who Labor. Mathew 11:28

Responsibility, with Wealth. Ecclesiastes 5:18

Wisdom, Knowledge, Riches. 2 Chronicles 1:11

Abuse, of what God, Gives. Ecclesiastes 6:1

Bishop, Must be blameless. Titus 1:7

Mockers, separated from God. Jude1:17

Angels, cast out from Heaven. Jude 1:6

Take the Right Pathway, or Pay. 3 John 1:11

Stay on Solid Ground. 2 Peter 3:17

Gods, Time, not Ours. 2 Peter 3:8

The Lord, knows how to Deliver us. 2 Peter 2:9

True Prophecy, only comes from God.

2Peter 1:20

Humble Yourself before God. 1 Peter 5:6

If any man Speaks Oracles of God. 1 Peter 4:11

Be of One Mind. 1 Peter 3:8

Honor, all men, fear God. 1 Peter 2:17

The Word, of the Lord, Endureth. 1 Peter 1:25

Be Holy, as Christ, is Holy. 1 Peter 1:16

The Trials, of your Faith. 1 Peter 1:7

My Rock, and Fortress, is the Lord. Psalms 18:2

The Words of My Mouth, be acceptable. Psalms 19:14

No Fear, God, is with Us. Isaiah 41:10

Swift to Hear, Slow to speak. James 1:19

Husband, and Wife, become One Flesh. Ephesians. 5:31

Study the Word, be Prepared. 2 Timothy 2:`15

Gods, Faithfulness to us. Joshua 1:5

Prodigal Son. Luke 15:11

Instruction, for Husbands, and Wives. Ephesians 5:22

Don't be Deceive with Vain Words.

Ephesians 5:6

Kind, to One another. Ephesians 4:32

Leave Old man, Put on New Man.

Ephesians 4:22

Spiritual Gifts. Ephesians 4:11

Ask, Pray, Believe. Mark 11:24

Temptations, are common to Man.

1 Corinthians 10:13

The Lord, is Faithful and True. Duet. 7:9

Gods, Security for Us. Hebrews 13:5

Mans, Wisdom is foolishness to God.

1 Corinthians 1:19

Gods, Assurance to us. 2 Corinthians 1:21

Made, in His Image. Genesis 1:26

The Heaven, declares the Glory of God.

Psalms 19:1

Let your Light shine before Men. Math.5:16

Humble yourself before God. T.L.B. James4:7-8

Wisdom, define by God, to us. James 3:13-18

We make Mistakes, James 3:1-6

Faith without Works, DEAD. James 2:17

Control your Tongue. T.L.B. James 1:26-27

Your, Identification. T.L.B. James 1:9-11

Gods, authority: Evil One. Mathew, 8:28

Speaking Lies. 1 Timothy 4:2

Ask, God, for Wisdom. James 1:5

Obedience, to the Lord. Proverbs 4:1

Apply, the Attributes of God. Proverbs 2:1

God, Gives Rest for Us. Mathew 11:28

Barron Mother, Joyful. Psalms 113:9

Function of the Body of Christ. Ephesians. 4:1

Be Ye Kind to One Another. Ephesians 4:32

Put off the Old Nature, On with the New nature Ephesians 4:22

The Inner Man be Strong. Ephesians 3:16

Our Foundation built on Christ. Ephesians.2:18

By Grace you are Saved. Ephesians. 2:8

Danger of the Human Tongue. James 3:5

Man, should show Meekness, and Wisdom James 3:13

What a Man, soweth, He shall Reap. Gal.6:7

Christ. Stands at the Door, Rev. 3:20

Be the same Mind, to one another. Rom.12:16

Nothing can Separate us from God's Love Romans 8:38

Definitions of Marriage: Math. 19:5

The Fear of the Lord, is Beginning of Wisdom. Psalms 111:10

Vengeance, is the Lords. Romans 12:9

Man, goes back to Dust. Ecclesiastes. 3:20

Definition of Prophet. Deuteronomy 13:1

Fear of the Lord, foundation of Life. Prov.14:27

Mans, ways are death. Proverbs 14:12

Seek the Lord, He may be found. Isaiah 55:6

Gods, attributes, comfort us. Psalms 23:4

Wait upon the Lord, for Renewal Isaiah 40:31

Seek those things above. Col. 3:1,9,16,23.

God, is the Creator Col.1:15

God's Purpose in everything. Ecclesiastes 3:1

No Sting in Death. 1 Corinthians 15:55

Paul's, Experience of Heaven.

2Corinthians 12:2-9

Perfect Love, cast on fear. 1 John 4:18

Your Request made Known to God. Philip.4:6

Forget things of the Past, reach to the future. Philippians 3:13

One Mediator, God. 1 Timothy 2:5,6.

Paul's, Life, before, after. 1 Timothy 12:13

Don't give Heed to Fables. 1 Timothy 1:4

Rejoice in the Lord, always Philippians 4:4

The Mind of Christ be in You. Philippians 2:5

Be Like minded in Christ. Philippians 2:2

God, begins a Good, Work in You. Phil. 1:6

Peace of God, Keeps you. Philippians 4:7

Trust the Lord. Psalms 16:1

God, will Judge all. 2 Timothy 4:1

Purpose of the Body of Christ. Heb. 10:25

Obedience of the Lord. Duet. 28:1-68

Holy Spirit, commands for Us. 2 Tim.1:7-8

The Holy Spirit, God's gift. T.L.B. 2 Tim. 1:7

God's, Creation Explanation, with Job. T.L.B. Job 38:4 etc.

Paul's, Purpose in the Church. 1 Corinthians 2:1-16

Holy Spirit, reveals to us all things. 1Corinthians 2:10

Count it all Joy, when you fall. James 1:2

Rejoice, in the Lord, Always Philippians 4:4

God, Leads us as Israel. Nehemiah 9:12

God's deliverance, from evil men. Psalms 140:1-6

Turn to the Right Direction. Gal. 1:8

Ask God, for Right Direction. James 1:6-7

All have Sinned. Romans 5:12

None Righteous, No Not One. Romans 3:10

Christ died for Us. Romans 5:8

All Have Sinned. Romans 5:12

Definition of Baptism: Romans 6:4

Holy Spirit, makes Intercession. Romans 8:26

Christ, is the only way to Heaven. Math. 7:21-27

The Trinity: 1 John 5:7

Christ, is the only way to Heaven. 1 John 5:11

Do not be Envious with Evil Men. Proverbs 24:1

Wisdom, and Strength comes from the Lord. Proverbs. 24:5a

Man's Religion, is in Vain, to God. James 1:26

Instructions for Christians. Math 5:-

Pride comes before the Fall. Proverbs 16:18

Wait on the Lord. Psalms 27:14

A fool says there is No God. Psalms 14:1

What do You Sow? 1Corinth. 15:42-44,49,50,52,54,55

A House, Divide does not Stand. Luke 11:17-23

Hide, The Word, In Your Heart, Psalms 119:11

Definition: Flesh and Spirit. 1Corinth. 15:39-50

Perfect Peace in Christ. Isaiah 26:3

Who is Lucifer? Isaiah 14:12-17

Without Christ's Love you have Nothing. 1Corinthians 13:----

God chose us, we did not choose Him. John 15:16

God's Wisdom Proverbs 1:7

Faith comes by Hearing. Romans 10:17

Printed in the United States
By Bookmasters